The Minimum JavaScript You Should Know

When You Code React & Redux

Tomy Jaya

1st Edition

Table of Contents

The Minimum JavaScript You Should Know When You Code React & Redux

About The Book

Well, okay, the title is a bit exaggerated. It should probably read *"The Recommended JavaScript You Should Know When You Code React & Redux"*. But then again, it will be less click-baity, less controversial, and most certainly generate less sales!

That aside, if you pick this book, chances are your team is migrating to React/ Redux or your architecture team has decided that the React/ Redux is the "strategic" UI framework to adopt for the enterprise.

You searched on Google for "react redux tutorial" and you found lots of JavaScript syntaxes alien (probably because you're from a Java/ C# background and the last time you coded JavaScript was a tiny validation script using JQuery in 2008). But that's no biggie! You embrace the virtue of continuous learning. You brag about: "I'm a polyglot developer yo!". And then, you decided to get several books on JavaScript: probably Eloquent JavaScript, JavaScript Allonge or even Understanding ES6. But Argh! they are all too verbose. Most of all, you are not a programming noob! You know what variables and conditional constructs are. You simply don't have time to waste on these basics. Well, I've been there too buddy. And that's why I wrote this pocket book (aka cheatsheet) to prep people like you transition quickly from basic JavaScript & intermediate programming knowledge to being able to productively follow through React/ Redux tutorials on the web.

Godspeed!

Prerequisites

Since this book will only cover subtleties & nuances of JavaScript, you should at least have the below prerequisites to follow along:

- Prior programming experience in any other programming language (e.g. knowledge of conditionals, loops, data types, etc.)
- Basic JavaScript syntax (incl. JSON)
- Basic Computer Science theories (e.g. immutability, data structure, arrays)
- How to run things in Chrome Dev Tools Console or Node.js environment (otherwise, you can't experiment with the code samples!)

Structure

The book will present JavaScript features accompanied by code examples, explanations, and occasionally exercises for you to check your understanding. I will also try to add snippets of React/ Redux code to illustrate where those features might be used in React/ Redux environment.

Contributing

If there's any material here which you believe is not accurate, let me know via Twitter @tomyjaya2.

Disclaimer

Finally, I have to say that most the examples I used are not my original work. The value I would like to bring is that of an aggregator and communicator, definitely not a thinker, let alone an inventor. Thus, where appropriate, I shamelessly copy pasted materials from online sources such as MDN and tried my best to credit them in the References section at the end of the book.

Acknowledgement

Special thanks to Hariharan Chandrasekar and @mohanmca for their help to proofread and edit this piece of writing.

Dedication

To Eric: May the passion to learn and share always be with you..

0. Data Types[1]

> JavaScript is a remarkably expressive dynamic programming language.
>
> - Doug Crockford (JavaScript Legend)

You might have heard that JavaScript is a **dynamically-typed** language. That means, types are bound to the **values** and determined only at **runtime**. That's very liberating if you come from Java/ C# background. Unlike in those **statically-typed** languages, JavaScript doesn't nag about assigning wrong types to wrong **variables** during **compile time**.

In this chapter, we'll examine powerful idioms made possible by this dynamic typing feature and conversely, several caveats to watch out for when 'exploiting' it.

Mixing different variable types

JavaScript has a nifty automatic type conversion feature. When you do operation on an "unexpected value", JavaScript will silently try to convert/ coerce the unexpected types to the ones it expects.

Let's see what happens if you mix 2 different types (e.g. `String` and `Number`):

```
console.log('10' + 20); //=> "1020"
```

Hmm.. It's quite intuitive. + acts as a concat method and as the first argument is `String` , JavaScript will convert the second one as `string` as well. What if we reverse it, though (i.e. `Number` + `String`):

```
console.log(10 + '20'); //=> "1020"
```

Whoa! It's still the same! We can still rationalize and say that `string` is somehow stronger than `Number` . Also, you might come from Java background and say that this is also in line with the behavior in Java. Just when you thought you got the hang of it:

```
console.log(10 * null) //=> 0
console.log("6" - 2) //=> 4
console.log("six" * 3) //=> NaN
console.log(false == 0) //=> true
```

Whoa Whoa Whoa! What's happening here? Rather than trying to explain the actual complicated and baffling rules deriving the above results, I'll just leave you with a quote and a meme[2]:

"Oh! It's just JavaScript being JavaScript.".

Hence, lessons to be learnt are:

1. Don't mix your types. It sometimes behaves intuitively, but other times, it doesn't. You don't want to end up spending countless hours debugging the latter scenario.
2. When there's no compiler to help you with types, unit test is your best friend.
3. Don't rely on JavaScript's automatic type conversion. You don't want to memorize all its rules and certainly should not expect the reader of your code to know of all of them by heart.

Type Coercion Comparison

There are 2 types of equality comparators in JavaScript: `==` (double equals) and `===` (triple equals).

The former will use automatic type conversion (type coercion) if the 2 operands are not of the same type:

```
console.log('6' == 6); //=> true
```

while the latter won't:

```
console.log('6' === 6); //=> false
```

You might think this `==` is an awesome convenience feature, but I will advise you against using it. Always use === (or !== for the inequality counterpart). Again, the reason is unpredictability:

```
console.log(false == 'false')    //=> false
console.log(false == '0')        //=> true
console.log(false == null)       //=> false
console.log(false == undefined)  //=> false

console.log('' == '0')           //=> false
console.log(0 == '')             //=> true
```

The lack of commutative & transitive properties will produce hard to trace bugs.

Truthy & Falsy value

Unlike in strongly typed languages, any values in JavaScript can be used as a boolean check. When JavaScript expect a boolean type but given a non-boolean type, JavaScript will convert it to its corresponding boolean value. A non-boolean value which converts to `true` is called truthy; otherwise, if it converts to `false` , it's called falsy.

```
const aTruthyNonBoolean = 'hello';

if (aTruthyNonBoolean) { // I can use string as a predicate!
  console.log('Whoa!');
} //=> 'Whoa!'
```

```
const aFalsyNonBoolean = '';

if (aFalsyNonBoolean) { // I can use string as a predicate!
  console.log('Not printed :(');
}
```

The below are some of the truthy or falsy values worth remembering:

JS Value	I.e.	Truthy or Falsy
{}	Empty Object	Truthy
[]	Empty Array	Truthy
''	Empty String	Falsy
0	Zero	Falsy
'0'	String with value Zero	Truthy
'false'	String with value false	Truthy
'true'	String with value true	Truthy

To easily find if a type is truthy or falsy, you can easily prefix the value with double exclamation marks (!!):

```
!!{} //=> true
!![] //=> true
!!'' //=> false
// ...
```

Short Circuit Operators

In JavaScript, the boolean && conjunction returns the right value if the left value is truthy. It will not evaluate the right operand if the left operand is falsy. It will just return the left operand itself. See example below:

```
// 1 is truthy, so, the right operand 'YO!' will be returned
1 && 'YO!' //=> YO!

// 0 is falsy, so it will return 0
// without even evaluating anUndefinedFunction()
0 && anUndefinedFunction() //=> 0
```

The behavior above gives rise to one of its most popular idioms: short circuit operator. Basically, instead of doing `null` or `undefined` check in an `if` guard, you can just use `&&` :

```
function funcWhichMightReturnNull(shouldReturnNull) {
  if (shouldReturnNull) {
    return null;
  } else {
    return {
      toPrint: 'print me'
    };
  }
}
const nullPrinter = funcWhichMightReturnNull(false);

// instead of verbose:
if (nullPrinter) {
  console.log(nullPrinter.toPrint);
}
// you can do:
console.log(nullPrinter && nullPrinter.toPrint); //=> print me


const stuffPrinter = funcWhichMightReturnNull(true);
// instead of verbose:
if (stuffPrinter) {
  console.log(stuffPrinter.toPrint);
}
// you can do:
console.log(stuffPrinter && stuffPrinter.toPrint); //=> null
                                    // (But No error/ exception)
```

You will see a lot of this in React as conditional rendering. E.g.

```
function Mailbox(props) {
  const unreadMessages = props.unreadMessages;
  return (
    <div>
      <h1>Hello!</h1>
      {unreadMessages.length > 0 &&
        <h2>
          You have {unreadMessages.length} unread messages.
        </h2>
      }
    </div>
  );
}
```

Defaulting

The `||` boolean conjunction behaves the opposite of `&&`. So, if the left operand is falsy, it will evaluate and return the right operand. If the left operand is truthy, it will just return it.

```
// Since 0 is falsy, it will return 'right'
0 || 'right' //=> right

// Since 1 is truthy, it will just return itself
1 || 'right' //=> 1
```

Similar to short circuit check, you will see this common idiom in JavaScript to provide default values:

```
function funcWhichMightReturnNull2(shouldReturnNull) {
  if (shouldReturnNull) {
    return null;
  } else {
    return 'Result';
  }
}

const test3 = funcWhichMightReturnNull2(false);
```

```
// instead of verbose:
if (test3) {
  console.log(test3); //=> Result
} else {
  console.log('function returns null');
}

// you can just do:
console.log(test3 || 'function returns null'); //=>  Result

const test4 = funcWhichMightReturnNull2(false);

// instead of verbose:
if (test4) {
  console.log(test4);
} else {
  console.log('fn returns null'); //=> fn returns null
}

console.log(test4 || 'fn returns null');
                          //=> fn returns null
```

Again, this defaulting is common in React. For instance, when setting default value for properties:

```
return (
    <button>{props.message || "Default text"}</button>
);
```

[1]. As array starts with index 0, I started this book with Chapter 0. ↵

[2]. Apparently, in 2018, the best way to convey your message is by using memes ↵

1. Scopes

> Ten days did not leave time for block scope. Also many 'scripting
> languages' of that mid-90s era had few scopes & grew more later.
>
> - Brendan Eich (Creator of JavaScript)

Importance of `var`

JavaScript has a `var` keyword which declares a variable within a function
scope.

```javascript
function getTotalSalary(type, baseSalary) {
  // GOOD: bonusMultiplier is only
  // available within this function scope
  // due to the var prefix
  var bonusMultiplier = {
    developer: 1.1,
    manager: 2,
    executive: 3.8
  };
  return baseSalary * bonusMultiplier[type];
}

getTotalSalary('developer', 4000); //=> 4400

getTotalSalary('executive', 40000); //=> 152000

console.log(bonusMultiplier); //=> ReferenceError:
                              // bonusMultiplier is not defined
```

JavaScript is quite lenient, though. If you forget the `var` prefix, JavaScript
will just attach your variable to the global scope. But as seen below, it's a poor
choice of default behavior:

```
function getTotalSalaryBad(type, baseSalary) {
  // BAD! no var means bonusMultiplier
  // is attached to the global scope
  bonusMultiplier = {
    developer: 1.1,
    manager: 2,
    executive: 3.8
  };
  return baseSalary * bonusMultiplier[type];
}

getTotalSalaryBad('developer', 4000); //=> 4400

// so far so good, but:

console.log(bonusMultiplier); //=> {
                              //      developer: 1.1,
                              //      manager: 2,
                              //      executive: 3.8
                              //   }
```

Whoa! `bonusMultiplier` is now available outside of the function! And more
importantly, we, developers, are so underpaid compared to the C-level
executives! Even compared to our managers, our bonus is peanuts! Time to
start a protest! :P

We can use strict mode to prevent this runtime issue, though. Instead of
attaching the variable to global scope, JavaScript in strict mode will default
non-var-prefixed variables to be undefined. We tell the JS compiler to use strict
mode by adding `'use strict';` expression at the top of our JS file:

```
'use strict';

function getTotalSalaryStrict(type, baseSalary) {
  bonusMultiplier = {
```

```
    developer: 1.1,
    manager: 2,
    executive: 3.8
  };
  return baseSalary * bonusMultiplier[type];
}

getTotalSalaryStrict('developer', 4000) //=> ReferenceError:
                                        // bonusMultiplier is not
defined

// consequently, bonusMultipler is not leaked out

console.log(bonusMultiplier); //=> ReferenceError:
                              // bonusMultiplier is not defined
```

In conclusion, if you forget to use `var` to declare your function scope, not only are you polluting/ cluttering the global namespace, you might also leak out confidential information. Using strict mode can prevent you from doing this. So, always use strict mode[1]

Hoisting

Declarations of `var` s are said to be "hoisted" in JavaScript. What it means is simple, when you do:

```
function hoistMe() {
  dosth();
  var a = 20;
  dosth();
}
```

what the JavaScript compiler will do is actually to bring up the var declaration to the top of the function:

```
function hoistMe() {
  var a; // Look Ma! declaration moved to the top!
```

```
    dosth();
    a = 20;
    doSth();
}
```

Notice that only the declaration is hoisted, not the assignment. This brings to a commonly followed style to always declare `var` s at the top of your function; because most JavaScript newbies are not aware of this feature.

In addition, you should know that function declarations are also hoisted. That's why I can invoke a function even before declaring it:

```
// invoke function
dosth(); //=> doing something

// declared below
function dosth() {
  console.log("doing something");
}
```

But function expressions are different, they are not hoisted:

```
dosth2(); //=> TypeError: dosth2 is not a function

var dosth2 = function dosth2() {
  console.log("doing something 2");
}
```

Style purists such as Doug Crockford argue that function expressions are the better way as relying on hoisting is seen as showing lack of discipline (aka sloppiness).

Exercise:

What would be printed in the below code?

```
printMe();
```

```
function printMe() {
  var a = 0;
  console.log(a);
  console.log(b);
  var b = 1;
  console.log(b);
  console.log(c);
}
```

Answer:

```
0
undefined
1
ReferenceError: c is not defined
```

Block Scope

I haven't fully emphasized the fact that `var` is function scoped:

```
// beware! var is function scoped!
function test() {
  // It seems that I'm declaring i only
  // within the for-loop block
  for (var i = 0; i < 10; i++) {
    console.log(i);
  }
  console.log('test: value of i: ' + i); // is it available here?
}
test(); //=> 0 ... 9
        //=> test: value of i: 10
        // Boy, was I wrong..
```

what actually happened was something like:

```
function test() {
  var i; // var is hoisted to the top of the function
```

```
for (i = 0; i<10; i++) {
  console.log(i);
}
console.log('test: value of i: ' + i); // obviously i is
                                        // still available here.

}
```

As of ES2015, there is an elegant solution for this problem. `let` and `const` are the keywords to define block scoped variables:

```
// use let instead
function test2() {
  for (let i = 0; i<10; i++) {
    console.log(i);
  }
  console.log('test2 -  i: ' + i); // i not available anymore
}
test2(); //=> 0 ... 9
          //=> Uncaught ReferenceError: i is not defined
          // This makes more sense...
```

The difference between `let` and `const` is as the name implies. `const` is a constant, and therefore, it doesn't allow re-assignment of values:

```
const person = "Nick";
person = "John"; // Will raise an error, person can't be reassigned


let person2 = "Nick";
person2 = "John";
console.log(person2); //=> John
                      // reassignment is allowed with let
```

Public Service Announcement (PSA): ditch `var` and always use `let` and `const` ! Before ES2015, JavaScript doesn't have any facility for block scoping and people were doing gymnastics such as IIFE to confine variable scopes. As

of 2015, JavaScript have modules and block scope variables which allows you
to easily achieve encapsulation. Utilize them!

Nested Scope

Scopes are nested as how you would expect in other languages. That is, a child
scope has access to its parent scope and child scope can shadow (create its own
copy of its parent's variables):

```javascript
function doA() {
  var a = 1;
  function doB() {
    var b = 2;
    console.log(b);
    console.log(a); // a is available from parent
  }
  doB();
  console.log(b); // b was only in doB()
}

doA(); // => 2
       // => 1
       // ReferenceError: b is not defined
```

```
// How about shadowing?
function doC() {
  var c = 3;
  function doD() {
    var d = 4;
    var c = 33; // let's try to shadow c
    console.log(d);
    console.log(c); // Guess what's printed???
  }
  doD();
  console.log(c);
}

doC(); // => 4
         // 33 (shadowing works!)
         // 3 (parent's variable is untouched!)
```

I only showed examples of `var` because for `let` , nested scope behavior is
pretty much as intuitive as other languages (e.g. C# or Java).

[1]. Preventing access to global variables is just one of the things strict
mode does. It also obliterates the use of `eval` , overriding of
`arguments` , and usage of `with` syntaxes. Basically, strict mode
prevents you from using confusing JavaScript features which you will
definitely regret in the future. ↵

2. Functions

> JavaScript is Lisp in C's Clothing
>
> - Doug Crockford (Still A JavaScript Legend)

JavaScript in its core is a functional language. Its support for functions is first-class [1].

Higher Order Functions

Higher order functions are functions which consume and/or return functions.

```javascript
// function returning a function
function f1() {
  return function() {
    console.log("anon function called");
  }
}

f1()(); //=> anon function called

function executeTwice(funcToExecute) {
  funcToExecute();
  funcToExecute();
}

executeTwice(function() {
  console.log('execute me twice!');
});
  //=> execute me twice!
  //=> execute me twice!
```

Currying & Composition

Being able to pass functions around gives rise to patterns of functional composition as a way to achieve re-use.

For example, in JavaScript, currying[2] is easy:

```
// non-curried add
function add(a,b) {
  return a + b;
}

add(2,5);

// curried add:
function add(a) {
  return function(b) {
    return a +b;
  }
}

const increment = add(1); // increment is a reusable function :)

console.log(increment(5)); //=> 6
console.log(increment(99)); //=> 100
```

To simplify things, you can think of React's Higher Order Components (function taking a component, and returning a component) as currying in practice. It's a pattern for re-use, by injecting cross-cutting concerns, through functional composition.

Currying is often associated with partial application. They are not exactly the same, though. The former always produces a nested unary functions, while the latter produces functions with arbitrary arity. The easiest way to understand the difference is by looking at RamdaJS[2]'s examples for both curry and partial :

```
var addFourNumbers = (a, b, c, d) => a + b + c + d;
```

```
// Create a curried version of the function
var curriedAddFourNumbers = R.curry(addFourNumbers);

var f = curriedAddFourNumbers(1, 2); // This is partial application

var g = f(3);
g(4); //=> 10
```

Formally, below is the example `partial` :

```
var multiply2 = (a, b) => a * b;
var double = R.partial(multiply2, [2]);
double(2); //=> 4

// or its other variant, partialRight:

var greet = (salutation, title, firstName, lastName) => salutation
 + ', ' + title + ' ' + firstName + ' ' + lastName + '!';
var greetMsJaneJones = R.partialRight(greet, ['Ms.', 'Jane', 'Jone
s']);
greetMsJaneJones('Hello'); //=> 'Hello, Ms. Jane Jones!'
```

The most common pattern to build re-usable functions is to curry an existing n-ary function, and using the curried version of that function, partially apply/ preload several arguments.

Exercise

Create a function called prepend, which can be invoked in curried-style. e.g.

```
const negate = prepend('un');
console.log(negate('happy')); //=> unhappy
```

Answer:

```
function prepend(prefix) {
```

```
  return function(content) {
    return prefix + content;
  }
}
```

Arrow Functions

Since ES 2015, there is shorter way to declare anonymous functions:

```
// pre-ES2015
const traditional = [1, 2, 3].map(function (x) {
  return x * 2;
});

console.log(traditional); //=> [2, 4, 6]

// ES2015
const arrow = [1, 2, 3].map((x) = { return x * 2; });
console.log(arrow); //=> [2, 4, 6]

// Or... // we can omit curlys and return if it's just a one line
expression

const arrowExpression = [1, 2, 3].map((x) => x* 2);
console.log(arrowExpression);
```

Anonymous and arrow functions are not exactly equivalent, though. For now,
you can take it that they can be replaced one-to-one; nonetheless, we will revisit
arrow functions again when we look at the `this` keyword binding in the later
chapters.

Collection Style Programming

Collection-style or Box-style programming is a popular way to make use of
higher order functions.

The cornerstone of this style of programming is understanding `map`, `filter`, and `reduce`.

1. `map` simply takes a function which will transform input to an output
2. `filter` simply takes a predicate function which should return a boolean value. `true` means the item is to be included, `false` means the item should be filtered out.
3. `reduce` is a bit harder to explain. I see it as a way to combine (aka fold) items in a collection one by one through a reducer function and accumulating the result as it goes through.

```
// pre-ES2015
const result0 = [1, 2, 3]
                .map(function(x) { return 2 * x;})
                .filter(function(x) { return x > 2; })
                .reduce(function(accu, curr) { return accu + cur
r;}, 0)
console.log(result0); //=> 10

// ES2015 - with arrow function
const result = [1, 2, 3]
               .map(x => 2 * x)
               .filter(x => x > 2)
               .reduce((accu, curr) => accu + curr, 0)
console.log(result); //=> 10
```

Since it's 2018, why *not* try to explain things in emoji?

```
map, filter, and reduce
explained with emoji 😂

map([🐮, 🍟, 🐔, 🥔], cook)
=> [🍔, 🍲, 🍗, 🍟]

filter([🍔, 🍲, 🍗, 🍟], isVegetarian)
=> [🍲, 🍟]

reduce([🍔, 🍲, 🍗, 🍟], eat)
=> 💩
```

Image credits: http://www.globalnerdy.com

`map` , `filter` , `reduce` might be difficult to understand at first, but once you get the hang of it, you'll forget other ways of manipulating collection without them!

Exercise:

You have an array of users

```
const users = [{gender:'M', age :20, name: 'John'}, {gender:'F', age: 21, name: 'Jenny'}];
```

use collection-style programming to return just the names of the female users.

Answer:

```
// pre-ES2015
```

```
users
  .filter(function(user) { return user.gender === 'F'; })
  .map(function(user) { return user.name; });

// ES2015
users
  .filter(u => u.gender === 'F')
  .map(u => u.name);
```

Collection-style programming is prominent in Redux as it provides convenient way to preserve immutability. For example, in Redux, if you want to display the list of to-dos which are pending, you would do:

```
const todos = [{task:'Buy Milk', isDone: false},
               {task:'Read Min JS', isDone: true}];

// GOOD
const pendingTodos = todos.filter(todo => !todo.isDone);

//instead of verbose mutation: (BAD!)
for(let i = todos.length - 1; i >= 0; i--) {
    if(todos[i].isDone) {
        todos.splice(i, 1);
    }
}
```

We'll discuss more about immutability in the next chapter.

Closure

Knowing what the term closure means is not required when coding basic React/ Redux apps; nevertheless, I got very annoyed when people use the term closure so loosely. The term closure is misunderstood so much in the React community until a point where people think a closure is synonymous to an arrow function.

No, people, closures are not the same as arrow functions. Closures are:

1. functions
2. who still have access to their parent's scope (fancy term: lexical environment)
3. even while their parent functions have already ended (exited)

Again, an example speaks more:

```
function makeCounter() {
  // counter variable lives in makeCounter's scope
  let counter = 0;
  return function() {
    // this anonymous function has access to counter
    return ++counter;
  }
  // 3. parent function (makeCounter) exits
}

const firstCounter = makeCounter();
// firstCounter is a closure!
// 1. it's a function

console.log(firstCounter()); //=> 1
console.log(firstCounter()); //=> 2
// 2. since it keeps incrementing,
// it's clear that variable counter is still retained

const secondCounter = makeCounter();
// new lexical environment means counter is reset
console.log(secondCounter()); //=> 1
```

In the example above, closure is used for information hiding (encapsulation). The variable counter is only privately accessible within the parent function. Access to it publicly has to go through the closure.

For example, we actually had seen closure in action in our currying example:

```
function makeAdder(x) {
  // x is a variable in the parent function scope
  return function(y) {
    // 2. x is accessible in this inner function
```

```
    return x + y;
  };
  // 3. parent function exits
}

var add5 = makeAdder(5);
// 1. add5 is a function
// add5 is a closure!

var add10 = makeAdder(10);
// So is add10!

console.log(add5(2));  // 7
console.log(add10(2)); // 12
```

See! We've been using closures without even knowing it! Closure is actually quite intuitive. In fact, without closure, reasoning about your code will be very hard!

Lastly, it's fine if you don't fully grasp what closure is. Just please, for the posterity's sake, stop spreading false definitions!

1. To quote MDN's Glossary: "A programming language is said to have First-class functions when functions in that language are treated like any other variable. For example, in such a language, a function can be passed as an argument to other functions, can be returned by another function and can be assigned as a value to a variable." ↵

2. Ramda is a functional-flavored library of utility functions. It's a must-have dependency in most JavaScript application. ↵

3. Inheritance

JavaScript is as related to Java as Carnival is to Car.

- Kyle Simpson (Author of You Don't Know JS)

Skippable Ramblings

You should have heard that JavaScript is a prototype-based language. Its mechanism of inheritance is through the prototypes chain (instead of classes hierarchy). Understanding how prototypical inheritance works in JS is essential. Sadly, though, people from Java/ C# or other class-based languages rarely invest their time to learn this paradigm. As a consequence, in ES2015, JavaScript introduced classes; which is merely a syntactic sugar to help people from the class-based inheritance camp to adopt JavaScript.

Many experts (incl. Doug Crockford) dislike the idea of introducing `class` es because it actually clouds the actual mechanics of how inheritance works in JavaScript. However, so many React tutorials out there use `class` es. (including the official guide!). So, instead of being a purist, I would decide to go for the pragmatic path. That is, let◆s look at how classes work in JavaScript

Classes

```
// Define a class Car
class Car {
  // constructor accepts 2 arguments
  // and assigning them as Car's properties
  constructor (brand, make) {
    this.brand = brand;
    this.make = make;
```

```
    }

    // define a method
    getDisplayName() {
      return `(${this.brand}) ${this.make}`;
    }
}
```

As seen above, syntax for defining a class is pretty similar to C#/ Java, except we don't need to worry about types and constructor uses the `constructor` keyword instead of the `class` name. Instantiating a class is equally similar:

```
// let's instantiate my favorite car:
const hondaJazz = new Car ('Honda', 'Jazz');
console.log (hondaJazz.getDisplayName()); //=> 'Honda Jazz'
```

I know, I know, you must be thinking: who in the right mind has Honda Jazz as his favorite car? Has he ever heard of Bugatti Veyron? Lamborghini Veneno? or Ferrari F60? But that's not important for now. What's more important is the fact that you can extend classes:

```
class AutoCar extends Car {

  getDisplayName() {
    return super.getDisplayName() + ' [Automatic Transmission]';
  }

}
```

You extend a class by using the `extends` keyword and you can easily override a super classes' method by declaring another method with the same signature. In case you need access to the super class' method, the keyword `super` is there to help.

Again, the syntax is eerily similar to Java, giving you the illusion that JavaScript inheritance is the same as Java's inheritance.

You can instantiate the subclass as seen below:

```
// the only car better than Honda Jazz is the Automatic version of
 Honda Jazz
const autoHonda Jazz = new AutoCar ('Honda', 'Jazz');
console.log(autoHonda Jazz.getDisplayName()); //=> 'Honda Jazz [Au
tomatic Transmission]'
```

Equipped with this knowledge of classes, the following React snippet should seem very familiar now (apart from the JSX which is out of scope of this book):

```
class HelloComponent extends React.Component {
  render() {
    return (<h1>Hello World</h1>);
  }
}
```

Explanation: `HelloComponent` is a subclass of `React.Component` and it overrides or declares a method called `render`. React Component is the main class in React. Extending it allows you to define behavior of React elements. For instance, to add a lifecycle hook when the component is mounted to the DOM, you can override the `componentDidMount` method:

```
class HelloComponent extends React.Component {
  render() {
    return (<h1>Hello World</h1>);
  }
  // override React's Lifecycle API
  componentDidMount() {
    console.log('Hello Component mounted to DOM');
  }
}
```

Final Notes

There are many good tutorials out there about JavaScript Prototypical inheritance. One I would recommend reading is Kyle Simpson's crisp book **You don't know JS: this & Object Prototypes**. It's available to read online for free in Github. You can also buy a copy of his book to support his work.

For completeness sake, below is the example in this chapter written the prototype way:

```
function Car(brand, make) {
  this.brand = brand;
  this.make = make;
}

Car.prototype.getDisplayName = function () {
  return `(${this.brand}) ${this.make}`;
}

function AutoCar(brand, make) {
  Car.call(this, brand, make);
}

AutoCar.prototype = Object.create(Car.prototype);
AutoCar.prototype.constructor = AutoCar;
AutoCar.prototype.getDisplayName = function() {
  return Car.prototype.getDisplayName.call(this) + ' [Automatic Tr
ansmission]';
}

const hondaJazz = new Car ('Honda', 'Jazz');
console.log(hondaJazz.getDisplayName()); //=> 'Honda Jazz'

const hondaJazzAuto = new ProtoAutoCar ('Honda', 'Jazz');
console.log (hondaJazzAuto.getDisplayName()); //=> 'Honda Jazz [Au
tomatic Transmission]'
```

It's obviously more verbose; nonetheless, it's very explicit that `AutoCar` inherits directly from an **Object** (`car`) through the virtue of the `prototype` chain.

4. Immutability

> The last thing you wanted any programmer to do is mess with internal
> state even if presented figuratively.
>
> - Alan Kay in The Early History of SmallTalk

You must have heard that immutability is of paramount importance in
multithreaded programming. However, since JavaScript is single-threaded
(more about this next chapter), does that mean immutability is pointless? No, if
you want to use Redux, you should know that an immutable state tree is at the
core of this framework. So, skip this chapter if you don't plan to use Redux, but
read on otherwise.

Arrays

```javascript
// How do we append item to an array?
var arrMutable = [1,2,3];
// Simple, use array.push!
arrMutable.push(4);
console.log(arrMutable); //=> [1, 2, 3, 4]
```

The above code is perfectly fine for most use cases. However, Redux state-tree
optimization relies on object reference check (===). This means that
modifying the existing array defeats the assumption that "if object reference is
same, the object is equal". So, a more redux friendly approach is to use array's
concat :

```javascript
var arrImmutable = [1,2,3];
var arrImmutableResult = arrImmutable.concat([4]);
```

```
console.log(arrImmutable);
              //=> [1, 2, 3] (Original array is intact!)
console.log (arrImmutableResult);
              //=> [1, 2, 3, 4]
```

Since ES2015, though, there is a shorter way to immutably append an item to an array. That is, by using the array spread operator (...):

```
const arr1 = [1, 2, 3];

// copy over everything from arr1
// and add 4 at the end.
const arr2 = [...arr1, 4];

console.log(arr1);
       //=> [1, 2, 3] (Original array is intact!)
console.log(arr2);
       //=> [1,2,3,4]
```

Objects

```
// How do we add an attribute to an object?
var person = {name: "Tomy" };
// Simple, just use the brackets notation!
person['gender'] = 'M';
console.log (person);
    //=> {name: "Tomy", gender: "M"}
```

Again, we are mutating the object which is unacceptable in Redux. The alternative to mutation is to create a new object and assign it with the properties of the old object, plus the new attributes.

```
// Better.. immutable
var originalPerson = {name: "Tomy" };
var personWithGender = Object.assign({}, originalPerson, {gender:
'M' });
```

```
console.log (originalPerson);
              //=> {name: "Tomy"} (Original object is intact!)
console.log (personWithGender);
              //=> {name: "Tomy", gender: "M"}
```

This `Object.assign` construct is rather verbose. I included this syntax since some old Redux tutorials still make use of it, though. Luckily, similar to array spread operator, ES7 has a more succinct alternative called *Object Spread Operator*.

In short, the ... (spread) notation, lets you copy over the properties of the old object:

```
// Let's define an object iPhone7

const iPhone7 = {
  version: 7,
  model: 'Iphone',
  ram: '2GB',
  batteryLifeInHours: 10,
  price: 700
};

// Apple launches annually, we need iPhone8

// But innovation runs dry,

// let's just copy iPhone7 and label it differently

// And hope customers don't realize it

const iPhone8 = {...iPhone7, version: 8};

// let's increase the price so that customers
// still think they are buying something new:

const iPhone8InMarket = {...iPhone7, version: 8, price: 1000};

console.log(iPhone7);
  //=> {version: 7, model: "Iphone", ram: "2GB", batteryLifeInHour
s: 10, price: 700}
```

```
  // original object intact!

 console.log(iPhone8);
   //=> {version: 8, model: "Iphone", ram: "2GB", batteryLifeInHour
 s: 10, price: 700}

 console.log(iPhone8InMarket);
   //=> {version: 8, model: "Iphone", ram: "2GB", batteryLifeInHour
 s: 10, price: 1000}
```

The above is purely for fun. No harm or foul intended. In fact, to be honest, I'm actually an Apple fanboy.

Conceptual Check!

Does using `const` guarantee immutability?

I'll let you think for a while..

Okay. Let's answer that question by using an easy counter example.

```
 const ben = { name: 'Ben Solo', alterEgo: 'Kylo Ren', affiliation:
 'Dark side' };

 console.log(ben); //=> {name: "Ben Solo", alterEgo: "Kylo Ren", af
 filiation: "Dark side"}

 // I can easily mutate ben below
 // there will be no error thrown by JS
 ben.affiliation = 'Light side';

 // And indeed! Rei is right! We could persuade Ben to come back to
  the way of the Jedi.
 console.log(ben); //=> {name: "Ben Solo", alterEgo: "Kylo Ren", af
 filiation: "Light side"}
```

In conclusion, NO! Using `const` doesn't mean that your data structure is safe from being mutated. It just means that it can't be reassigned to another item. The item itself, though, can be easily altered. Don't mix immutability the `const` !

Apologies for those who don't get the Star Wars reference, though.

Exercise

Use Object spread operator to fill in the `Fill me` branch below:

```javascript
// state is defined as
const state = {
  name: 'Bob',
  gender: 'M'
}

// action has this shape:
const action = {
  type: 'CHANGE_NAME',
  name: 'Tomy'
}

// We have a reducer function which accepts state and action
function reducer (state, action) (
  // If the action's type is CHANGE_NAME,
  // I should return a new state with name modified to be
  // action's name
  if (action.type === 'CHANGE_NAME') {
    // --- Fill me ---
  } else {
    return state;
  }
}

// Expected result:
console.log(reducer(state, action)); //=> {name:'Tomy',gender:'M'}
```

Answer:

```
return {...state, name: action.name);
```

Notes on performance

What if your object is large? Or your array contains millions of items? Copying them over everytime you need some change seems like a terribly bad performance idea right? That's true. But fret not, there are libraries like Mori and Immutable JS which can help you avoid this performance penalty by employing advance techniques of Persistent Data Structure. So if you ever find that your object or array grows too large and your profiling shows copying them over and over is the bottleneck, do check out those libraries.

5. Async

> Think like a fundamentalist. Code like a hacker.
>
> - Erik Meijer (inventor of Async/ Await multiple programming languages)

Hard prerequisites:

Event loop is the concurrency model adopted by JavaScript. I will now outsource the explanation of how the event loop works to the guy who does this best, Philip Roberts: What the heck is the event loop anyway?

Do not, I repeat, do not continue reading without watching the above video!

Quiz:

To check your understanding of the event loop, let's have a small quiz. What would the below print out?

```javascript
(function() {
  console.log(1);
  setTimeout(function() {console.log(2); }, 1000);
  setTimeout(function() {console.log(3); }, 0);
  console.log(4);
})();
```

Answer:

```javascript
//=> 1
//=> 4
```

```
//=> 3
//=> 2 (1 second later)
```

If you still don't understand why? I'd advice you to re-watch the event loop video recommended above.

Now that you've understood the mechanics underlying concurrency in Javascript, let's evaluate the many syntaxes JavaScript offers to achieve concurrency:

1. Callback
2. Promise
3. Async-Await

We'll look at the free weather API here: https://www.metaweather.com/api/ as a worked example. Our objective is to get the weather forecast for a city (e.g. Singapore). To do so, we require 2 steps:

1. Use `/api/location/search/?query=(query)` endpoint to query the `woeid` (where on earth id) of our city.
2. Use `/api/location/(woeid)` endpoint to get the weather details.

Callback

The most popular way to handle asynchrony in JavaScript is via a callback function. JQuery is the most commonly used callback-based AJAX library:

```
var city = 'Singapore';
var localSearchUrlPrefix = 'https://www.metaweather.com/api/locati
on/search/?query=';
var locationUrlPrefix = 'https://www.metaweather.com/api/location/'
;

jQuery.ajax({
  url: localSearchUrlPrefix + city,
  success: function(result) {
    console.log('woeid: ' + result[0]['woeid']);
```

```
   jQuery.ajax({
     url: locationUrlPrefix + result[0]['woeid'] + '/',
     success: function (result) {
       console.log('Result:', result.consolidated_weather);
       console.log('Weather today:', result.consolidated_weather[0
].weather_state_name);
     }
   });
 }
}); //=> woeid: 1062617
    //=> Result: <...>
    //=> Weather today: <...>
```

As seen above, callback has a problem: it nests rightward. As my call dependencies increase, nesting will become more cumbersome. This particular issue with deep nesting of callback is known as ***callback hell*** or the ***Christmas tree problem*** ('coz the jagged left indentation looks like a Christmas tree). A meme to describe the above problem can be found below:

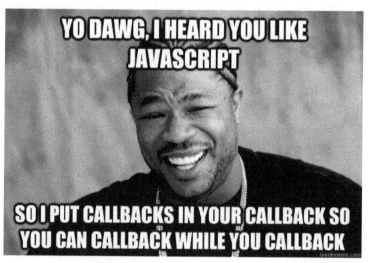

Promise To the Rescue

Luckily there exist a better library now to handle ajax: `fetch` . You can think of fetch as jQuery's ajax which is Promise-based (i.e. when you use `fetch` , you don't need to pass in a callback function as an argument, instead, you receive a `Promise` as the returned value).

`Promise` is just like callback, except that you pass the callback function by invoking a `.then` function of the promise. The `.then` is chainable as it wraps the return again in a `Promise` . It is such a powerful construct as `then` can unnest (i.e. flatten) nested promises. In the functional programming jargon, `Promise` is a Monad (did I just say the M-word?).

That aside, below is the callback example above in promise-style:

```
let city = 'Singapore';
let localSearchUrlPrefix = 'https://www.metaweather.com/api/locati
on/search/?query=';
let locationUrlPrefix = 'https://www.metaweather.com/api/location/'
;

fetch(localSearchUrlPrefix + city)
  .then((response) => response.json()) // you need to explicitly
                                        // get the JSON body
  .then((result) => {
    console.log('woeid: ' + result[0]['woeid']);
    // returning Promise inside a Promise below
    return fetch(locationUrlPrefix + result[0]['woeid'] + '/');
  })
  .then((response) => response.json()) // indeed having to do this

                                        // is quite annoying..
  .then((result) => {
    console.log('Result:', result.consolidated_weather);
    console.log('Weather today:', result.consolidated_weather[0].w
eather_state_name);
  });
  //=> woeid: 1062617
  //=> Result: <...>
  //=> Weather today: <...>
```

As seen above, the code with Promise expands top-to-bottom as Promise of Promise can be flattened with just one `then` invocation. The benefit of Promise will even be more obvious as the number of dependent ajax calls grows. While in the case of callback, code indents from left to right, Promise will chain top to bottom.

Another important thing you need to be aware of when using Promises is how to handle errors. Errors can come in 2 flavors: a `reject` ed Promise or a vanilla JavaScript `throw` statement:

```javascript
const promise1 = new Promise((resolve, reject) => {
  reject('Promise Rejection Error!');
});

promise1.then(() => {
  console.log("I am not executed");
});

const promise2 = new Promise((resolve, reject) => {
  throw 'Usual JS Error!';
});

promise2.then(() => {
  console.log("I am not executed");
});
```

In the above code example, both of the `then` blocks are not executed when the errors occurred. In a large codebase with long chained promises spanning across multiple functions, this can be a debugging nightmare. That is why people usually add a `catch` function handler at the end of your promise chain which works similar to the catch-all try-catch block. For example:

```javascript
let brokenUrl = 'http://a.broken.url';

fetch(brokenUrl)
  .then((response) => response.json())  // net::ERR_NAME_NOT_RESOLVED
  .then((result) => {
```

```
    console.log('result: ' + result);
  })
  .catch((err) => console.log('Caught an error: ' + err));
      // Caught an error: TypeError: Failed to fetch
```

Having a `catch` block is highly recommended to avoid the dreaded `unhandledpromiserejectionwarning`. Moreover, in the future release of node.js, unhandled rejected promises might lead to your process existing with a non-zero exit code!

Bear in mind that the `catch` block only "covers" or "protects" the regions before it:

```
let validUrl = 'https://www.google.com';
let brokenUrl = 'https://a.broken.url';

fetch(validUrl)
  .then((response) => response.text())
  .then((result) => {
    console.log('result: ' + result);
  })
  .catch((err) => console.log('Caught error: ' + err))
  .then(() => {
    return fetch(brokenUrl); // This portion is uncaught!
  });
```

That being said, I would still recommend putting some intermediate `catch` blocks with one ultimate `catch` -all block at the end of your Promise chain. The reason being: the intermediate `catch` blocks, coupled with proper logging, can help you narrow down which Promise block is the actual source of the error.

Async/Await

Async/Await is another addition to the JavaScript's concurrency arsenal (circa ES7). Async/ Await should not be alien to readers who are C#, Python, or Kotlin developers. In fact, JavaScript Async/Await's syntax is remarkably similar to the stated languages (probably because Erik Meijer is behind all of them?). Anyways, suppose we have the below code in Promise-based style:

```javascript
function resolveAfter1Second(x) {
  return new Promise((resolve) => {
    setTimeout(() => {
      resolve(x);
    }, 1000);
  });
}

function addTraditional() {
  return resolveAfter1Second(20)
    .then((a) => resolveAfter1Second(30)
        .then((b) =>  a + b)
    );
}

addTraditional().then(console.log);
                    //=> 50 (2 seconds later)
```

We can rewrite it in Async/ Await style as follows:

```javascript
async function addAsyncAwait() {
  const a = await resolveAfter1Second(20);
  const b = await resolveAfter1Second(30);
  return a + b;
}

addAsyncAwait() .then(console.log);
                  //=> 50 (2 seconds later)
```

There is no doubt the above code reads clearer. Async await is indeed the way of the future. Nevertheless, its underlying mechanism still relies on Promises (and Generators). Moreover, plenty of React articles out there still use

Promises. Thus, knowing how Promise works is still essential.

Internally, there's no runtime level magic in Async Await. The `async` keyword indicates that the compiler needs to wrap the function's return value in a `Promise`. The `await` keyword will then wait until the async function's return value resolve and assign the result to the variable on the left. As a result, the code reads as if things are happening sequentially.

One last note: the above example still resolves after 2 seconds. What if I want it to execute in parallel and end in 1 second? Well, for that, we need the help of our good friend, `Promise.all`:

```
async function addAsyncAwaitParallel() {
  const results = await Promise.all([resolveAfter1Second(20),
                                     resolveAfter1Second(30)]);
  return results[0] + results[1];
}

addAsyncAwaitParallel().then(console.log);
                            //=> 50 (1 second later)
```

Let's wrap up this chapter with an exercise.

Exercise:

Rewrite the Promise-based weather example in Async/ Await style.

Answer:

```
let city = 'Singapore';
let localSearchUrlPrefix = 'https://www.metaweather.com/api/locati
on/search/?query=';
let locationUrlPrefix = 'https://www.metaweather.com/api/location/'
;

let response1 = await fetch(localSearchUrlPrefix + city);
let result1 = await response1.json();
```

```
console.log('woeid: ' + result1[0]['woeid']);

let response2 = await fetch(locationUrlPrefix + result1[0]['woeid'
] + '/');
let result2 = await response2.json();
console.log('Result: ', result2.consolidated_weather);
console.log('Weather today:', result2.consolidated_weather[0].weat
her_state_name);
    //=> woeid: 1062617
    //=> Result: <...>
    //=> Weather today: <...>
```

6. Module

> Write programs that do one thing and do it well. Write programs to work together. Write programs to handle text streams, because that is a universal interface.
>
> - The Unix Philosophy

Before I start the discussion about modules, I have the confession to make. I, myself, still get confused by it. Unlike in Java/ C# (where you can just auto-import stuffs), working with JavaScript's module is still mostly manual (I don't recall Visual Studio Code has the feature to optimize imports yet). Moreover, module has been a hot debate topic causing its proposals and implementations to have been revised numerously. So, to avoid confusion, let's start with a history lesson, shall we?

IIFE (Immediately Invoked Function Expression)

In the olden days, there is no way to encapsulate pieces of JavaScript code together in a module. Ben Alman noticed that functions can be used to encapsulate scope and proposed that very way to simulate 'module pattern'. IIFE is short for Immediately Invoked Function Expression. As the name imply, it's a function expression (i.e. `(function() { ... })`) and it's immediately invoked (i.e. `()` suffix) . Let's see the example below:

```
(function() {
  var a = "1";
```

```
    var b = "2";
    console.log(a + b);
})();
    //=> 3
```

Neither `a` nor `b` are available outside of the function anymore. In a sense, we've achieved modularity.

Since IIFE was the only way to hide variable access in the past, the world of JavaScript is rampant with the above idioms. Another pattern is to leverage on closure to create module which can expose selective functions/ attributes, appropriately named as the Revealing Module Pattern:

```
var counter = (function() {
    // your module code goes here
    var sum = 0 ;

    return {
        add: function() {
            sum = sum + 1;
            return sum;
        },
        reset: function() {
            return sum = 0;
        }
    }
})();

console.log(counter.add()); //=> 1
counter.reset(); //=> 0
```

CommonJS

Node.js came along and as any other server-side solution, support for modularity is a must. Node's module implementation is based on CommonJS specification. In a nutshell, CommonJS has:

1. `exports` variable to expose module contents
2. a `require` function to declare your dependencies

So, for example, we can define the below module in a file called `mod1.js` :

```
// ----- mod1.js -----

// define 2 functions
const myFunc1 = function(){ console.log('myFunc1');};
const myFunc2 = function(){ console.log('myFunc2');};

// expose the above 2 functions
module.exports.myFunc1 = myFunc1;
module.exports.myFunc2 = myFunc2;

// module.exports is aliased as exports,
// so the below also works:
exports.myFunc1 = myFunc1;
exports.myFunc2 = myFunc2;
```

Now that these functions are exposed, we can use them in `mod2.js` as long as we declare our dependencies:

```
// ----- mod2.js -----

const mod1 = require('./mod1'); // omit the .js suffix!

mod1.myFunc1(); //=> myFunc1
mod1.myFunc2(); //=> myFunc2
```

We can also export classes as classes are just syntactic sugar for functions anyway:

```
// ----- Person.js -----

class Person {
  constructor(name) {
    this.name = name;
  }
}
```

```
  sayHello() {
    // search about JavaScript Template Literals
    // if you're amazed with the below syntax.
    console.log(`Hello! I am ${this.name}. `);
  }
}

module.exports = Person;
```

Again, depending on this class is a matter of specifying your dependency in the `require` function:

```
const Person = require('./Person'); // another reminder: omit the
.js suffix!
const bob = new Person('Bob');
bob.sayHello(); //=> Hello I am Bob
```

Many React examples will use this way to declaring module dependencies and now you know how to decipher those examples :)

AMD (Asynchronous Module Definition)

Folks on the browser-side were not satisfied with CommonJS, though. Specifically, they complained about the lack of asynchronous loading support in the browser environment. That's why they decided to fork commonJS and created a new module API called Asynchronous Module Definition (AMD). One implementation of AMD is RequireJS. You will rarely encounter React examples using RequireJS, though. It is simply because by the time React came about, module bundler such as Webpack rose to fame and Webpack doesn't favor this RequireJS syntax. Nevertheless, for completeness sake, I'll show a snippet for AMD:

```
define('module/id/string', ['module', 'dependency', 'array'],
  function(module, factory function) {
```

```
    return ModuleContents;
  });
```

The key addition is the `define` function which takes 3 arguments:

1. module name
2. array of module dependencies
3. function defining the module body.

The JS/ ES6/ ES2015 Module

ES6 module relies on 2 keywords: `import` & `export` . Let's look at the simplest example, *default export/ import*.

Default Export/ Import

Each module can only have one default export, you can define it as follows [1]:

```
// ----- lpad.js -----
export default function lpad(val, len, pad) {
    return (val.toString().length < len)
            ? lpad(pad + val, len, pad)
            : val;
}
```

importing this default export is as simple as:

```
// ----- main.js -----

import lpad from './lpad';

lpad('5',5,'0'); //=> 00005
```

Notice that since it's a default export, the "imported name" doesn't really matter. As seen below, you can assign the imported function as any other name:

```
// ----- main2.js -----

import leftPad from './lpad';

leftPad('10',5,'0'); //=> 00010
```

Classes and expressions can also be exported:

```
// ----- Person.js -----
export default class Person {
    // ... same as the CommonJS example
}

// ------ Numbers.js -----

// exporting
export default 7*5;
```

Now we can easily import them:

```
import Person from './Person';

const tim = new Person('Tim');
tim.sayHello(); //=> Hello! I am Tim.

import someNumber from './Numbers';
console.log(someNumber); //=> 35
```

This pattern of using default export is common in React, especially in stateless functional components:

```
// ----- Header.js -----
import React from 'react';

const Header = () => {
  return (<pre>The Most Concise JS Book</pre>);
};

export default Header;
```

Named Export/ Import

Another flavor of ES6 module is *named export/ import*. See the example below:

```
// ----- Constants.js -----
export const pi = 3.14;

export const e = 2.71;
```

The user of this constants can import them (notice the curly braces!):

```
import {pi} from './Constants';
import {e} from './Constants';

console.log(pi); //=> 3.14
console.log(e); //=> 2.71
```

There are 2 notable differences between named imports and default imports:

1. the curly braces (it's mandatory)
2. the name of the variable you import should match the actual one you export.

Hence, the below won't work:

```
import {euler} from './Constants'; // It won't work!
```

If you really need to name it as another variable, there is an `as` keyword to help you:

```
import {e as euler} from './Constants';
```

Finally, if you want to import all exported items from a module, you can use
* wildcard import:

```
import {* as constants} from './Constants';

console.log(constants.pi); //=> 3.14
console.log(constants.e); //=> 2.71
```

Mixing Named and Default Export/ Import

Finally, ES6 supports ways to mix named and default export/ import. It's not
that hard to figure out the syntax once you know each of them individually:

```
// ----- React.js -----

// Named export
export class Component {
    // ...
}


// Default export
export default {
    Component,
    PureComponent,
    createElement,
    // ...
}

// ----- yourClass.js ----

// React is default import, Component is a named import
import React, {Component} from 'react';
```

Do note that in the examples above, the convention I used when importing is to
remove the .js extensions. It is a common practice to do this in the React
world since most of the time, we rely on module bundlers such as Webpack or
Parcel to fill in the default extension. Nevertheless, do note that if you want to

use import/ export natively in browsers or in node's experimental feature, extensions are mandatory. In that case, the convention is to name module files `.mjs` to differentiate them from normal `.js` files.

Exercise

Convert the below CommonJS-based modules to ES2015:

```
// ----- lib.js -----
function add(a,b) {
  return a + b;
}
function multiply(a,b) {
  return a * b;
}

module.exports = {
  add: add,
  multiply: multiply
}

// ----- main.js -----
var lib = require('./lib');
console.log(lib.add(10,20)); //=> 30
console.log(lib.multiply(10,20)); //=> 200
```

Answer:

Since it's a multiple export, default exports will not cut it.

```
// ----- lib.js -----
export function add(a,b) {
  return a + b;
}
export function multiply(a,b) {
  return a * b;
}
```

I chose to use wildcard import below, but a selective named imports will also do:

```
// ----- main.js -----
import {* as lib} from './lib';

console.log(lib.add(10,20)); //=> 30
console.log(lib.multiply(10,20)); //=> 200
```

[1]. This example alludes to the infamous left-pad npm module fiasco in 2016. Basically, what happened was that this tiny npm module is depended upon by numerous other libraries. One fine day, the author decided that he wanted to remove this module from the npm repository and thousands of fragile builds started breaking. Luckily, npm is now fixed to prevent this disasterous event from reoccurring. The original `left-pad` code is obviously more elaborate as it covers more corner cases. I personally like this recursive version more, though. ↩

7. Language Quirks & Features

Fools ignore complexity. Pragmatists suffer it. Some can avoid it.
Geniuses remove it.

- Alan Jay Perlis (First Recipient of the Turing Award)

this

If I were to choose one most mystical feature of JavaScript, I would have to go
with `this` binding. It's because it has so many rules on how `this` variable is
resolved (pun intended). Let's go through all the rules:

implicit/ dot binding

When invoked on an object, this is bound to the object's on the left of the dot.

```
function sayName() {
  console.log('Hello I am ' + this.name);
}

const ben = {
  name: 'Ben',
  sayName: sayName
};

ben.sayName(); //=> Hello I am Ben
// this is bound to object ben


const bob = {
  name: 'Bob',
  friend: ben,
```

```
  sayName: sayName
};

bob.sayName(); //=> Hello I am Bob
// this is bound to object bob
bob.friend.sayName(); //=> Hello I am Ben
// this is bound to object bob.friend which is ben
```

new binding

The new keyword creates a new lexical scope.

```
class Car {
  constructor (brand, make) {
    this.brand = brand;
    this.make = make;
  }

  getDisplayName() {
    return `(${this.brand}) ${this.make}` ;
  }
}


const hondaJazz = new Car ('Honda', 'Jazz');
// hondaJazz now has its own lexical scope

console.log(hondaJazz.getDisplayName()); //=> (Honda) Jazz
```

Explicit binding (apply , bind , call)

You can explicit bound this by using helper functions apply , bind , or call :

```
function greet(isLoud) {
  if (isLoud) {
    console.log('YOYOYOYO! I am ' + this.name + '!!!');
  } else {
    console.log('Hi, I am ' + this.name);
```

```
  }
}

console.log('// apply - a for array')
greet.apply(ben, [true]); //=> YOYOYOYO! I am Ben!!!

console.log('// call ');
greet.call(ben, false); //=> Hi, I am Ben

console.log('// bind');
const benGreeting = greet.bind(ben);
benGreeting(true); //=> YOYOYOYO! I am Ben!!!
```

Quiz

Let's test our understanding with an example:

```
var batman = {
  _name: 'Bruce Wayne',
  getSecretIdentity: function() {
    return this._name;
  }
}

var stealIdentity = batman.getSecretIdentity;
// stealIdentity's lexical scope is now empty.
// How can we make this point to batman?


// i.e. How to make the below stealIdentity work?
console.log(stealIdentity()); //=> should be: 'Bruce Wayne'
```

Answer

```
console.log(stealIdentity.bind(batman)()); // bind returns a funct
ion, and we immediately invoke it.
// OR:
console.log(stealIdentity.apply(batman));
// OR:
console.log(stealIdentity.call(batman));
```

Note that since `getSecretIdentity` doesn't require any argument, the solution using `apply` and `call` look exactly the same.

Global/ Window Binding

Finally, if this is invoked at the top level scope, it will be assigned with the global/ window object:

```
function useThis() {
  console.log(this);
}

useThis(); //=> window in the browser, global in Node
```

Lexical Scope of Arrow Function vs. Normal Function

Throughout the examples in this book, it should come to your attention that **functions create new lexical scopes**. This is very much true for `this` keyword too. When you use the `function` keyword, new lexical environment (with its own `this` and `arguments` object).

Arrow functions are exempt from this rule, though. Since arrow function was initially designed to be lightweight, it's just right that it doesn't need their own lexical scope (i.e. can borrow from its parents).

Let's try to discern this with an example:

```
const mark = {
  name: 'Mark',
  friends: [{name: 'Eduardo'}, {name: 'Dustin'}],
  listFriends: function() {
    this.friends.forEach(function(friend) {
      // ----- FIX ME -----
      // If I uncomment the below,
      // the compiler will say that this is undefined:
      //
```

```
      // this.greetFriend (friend.name); });
   });
  },
  greetFriend: function(name) {
    console.log('Hi ' + name + "!");
  }
}


// I want the below to work:
mark.listFriends(); // => Hi Eduardo !
                    // => Hi Dustin!


// How to fix the above?
// 1. self = this
listFriends: function() {
   const self = this;
   this.friends.forEach (function (friend) {
       self.greetFriend (friend.name);
   });
 }


// 2. use arrow function since it uses parent's lexical scope
listFriends: function() {
  this.friends.forEach((friend) => (
    this.greetFriend (friend.name);
  });
}


// 3. use bind
listFriends: function() {
  const greetFriend = this.greetFriend.bind(this);
    this.friends.forEach(function(friend) {
      greetFriend(friend.name);
    });
}
```

Quiz

What will be printed below?

```
var myObject = {
  foo: 'bar',
  func: function() {
    var self = this;
    console.log("outer func: this.foo = " + this.foo);
    console.log("outer func: self.foo = " + self.foo);
    (function() {
      console.log("inner func: this.foo = " + this.foo);
      console.log("inner func: self.foo = " + self.foo);
    })(); // IIFE
  }
};

myObject.func();
```

Answer

```
//=> outer func: this.foo = bar
//=> outer func: self.foo = bar
//=> inner func: this.foo = undefined
//=> inner fung: self.foo = bar
```

Automatic Semi-colon Insertion

Let's say we have the below function:

```
function foo1() {
  return {
    bar: "hello"
  };
}
```

But, you know, people have different formatting preferences:

```
function foo2()
{
```

```
    return
    {
      bar: "hello"
    };
  }
```

This seems pretty harmless. But let's look at what actually happens when we invoke these 2 functions:

```
console.log("foo1 returns: ");
console.log(foo1()); //=> {bar: "hello"}
console.log("foo2 returns:");
console.log(foo2() ); //=> undefined!!
```

Oops! You've just become the victim of JavaScript's Automatic Semicolon Insertion feature. The second function is actually interpreted as such:

```
function foo2()
{
  return; // JS ASI in Action!
  // The lines below are dead/ unreachable code
  {
    bar: "hello"
  };
}
```

We all agree ASI is terrible idea, it promotes sloppy coding practices. Nevertheless, it's been there in JS since its inception. We can only work around it by: *Always using K&R curly braces style* (i.e. the former function)[1].

Object Property Shorthand

Suppose you have the below code:

```
const func1 = () => console.log('Yay!');
const var1 = 'abc';

const objOld = {
  func1: func1,
  var1: var1
};

console.log(objOld);
  //=> { func1: [Function: func1], var1: 'abc' }
```

As the names of the object's property and the variable are the same, you can omit repeating the declaration and assignment:

```
const objPropertyShorthand = {
  func1,
  var1
}

console.log(objPropertyShorthand);
  //=> { func1: [Function: func1], var1: 'abc' }
```

Exercise:

The below function should return an object with below properties:

1. type: 'CHANGE_NAME'
2. name: <name_in_the_argument>

```
function onChangeName(name) {
  // ---- Fill me -----
}

const changeToTomy = onChangeName('Tomy');
console.log(changeToTomy); // should be:
                      //=> {type: 'CHANGE_NAME', name: 'Tomy'
  }
```

Answer:

Just return the object literal, as a small optimization, use object property shorthand for `name` .

```
return {
  type: 'CHANGE_NAME',
  name // Object Property Shorthand
}
```

Destructuring Operator

The below example illustrates a new convenience feature of JavaScript, Destructing Operator:

```
const inputTuple = [1, 2];

function addTwoNumbers ([a, b]) {
  return a + b;
}
console.log(addTwoNumbers(inputTuple));

var o= { p: 42, q: true };
var { p, q } = o;
// var p = o.p;
// var q = o.q ;
console.log(p); //=> 42
console.log(q); //=> true

var o2 = { p: 42, q: true };
var { p: foo, q: bar } = o2;

console.log(foo); //=> 42
console.log(bar); //=> true
```

ES6 Map

In the first example of Chapter 1 (Scope), we saw how a plain JavaScript object literal can be used as a map/ hashtable/ dictionary. This has always been the case until ES6 introduced built-in `Map` data structure.

The previous example can be written as follows:

```
function getTotalSalary(type, baseSalary) {
  var bonusMultiplier = new Map();
  bonusMultiplier.set('developer',1.1);
  bonusMultiplier.set('manager',2);
  bonusMultiplier.set('executive',3.8);

  // Alternatively, Map has a constructor which accepts a 2d-array
  // var bonusMultiplier = new Map([['developer',1.1], ['manager',
2], ['executive',3.8]]);

  return baseSalary * bonusMultiplier.get(type);
}

getTotalSalary('developer', 4000); //=> 4400

getTotalSalary('executive', 40000); //=> 152000
```

The primary benefit of using this `Map` that you will get access to many convenience methods such as `.size()` , `.clear()` , `.forEach(fn)` , `.keys()` , `.values()` , `.entries()` for free. That being said, I haven't seen many examples of Redux reducers being written using `Map` s. Instead, people actually still prefer to use the good-old `switch-case` . Dan Abramov (creator of Redux) mentioned that using the built-in ES6 `Map` is not recommended as they are optimized for mutability. A better choice would be to use ImmutableJS's Map equivalent.

Object.freeze

Again, let's us revisit Chapter 1 (Scope)'s example. In that example, it was shown how without using `var` keyword, we have leaked the object to the global namespace.

Let's say that we don't mind making the `bonusMultiplier` public:

```javascript
var bonusMultiplier = {
    developer: 1.1,
    manager: 2,
    executive: 3.8
};

function getTotalSalaryBad(type, baseSalary) {
  return baseSalary * bonusMultiplier[type];
}
```

Another vulnerability of that code snippet is that the JavaScript object is actually mutable. So, someone could actually still modify the values as follows:

```javascript
getTotalSalaryBad('developer', 4000); //=> 4400

// let's increase developer's salary!
bonusMultiplier['developer'] = 10;

getTotalSalaryBad('developer', 4000); //=> 40000
```

To prevent this, JavaScript has a built-in `Object.freeze` method which accepts an object and return a frozen version of that object. Frozen here means, nothing can be added, changed, or removed.

```javascript
var safeBonusMultiplier = Object.freeze({
    developer: 1.1,
    manager: 2,
    executive: 3.8
});

function getTotalSalarySafe(type, baseSalary) {
  return baseSalary * safeBonusMultiplier[type];
```

```
}

// let's attempt to increase developer's salary!
safeBonusMultiplier['developer'] = 10;

getTotalSalarySafe('developer', 4000); //=> 4400

// Oh no, our attempt failed! It's still the same. :(
```

In strict mode, the error will be more explicit:

```
'use strict';
var safeBonusMultiplier = Object.freeze({
  developer: 1.1,
  manager: 2,
  executive: 3.8
});

function getTotalSalarySafe(type, baseSalary) {
  return baseSalary * safeBonusMultiplier[type];
}

// let's attempt to increase developer's salary!
safeBonusMultiplier['developer'] = 10;

// => Uncaught TypeError: Cannot assign to read only property
//                         'developer' of object '#<Object>'
```

[1]. Most JS linters will notify you of this type of error nowadays. ↵

8. Epilogue

One of the reasons why the community loves React is the fact that when they learn React, they are learning more JavaScript than just framework specific hooks and directives (e.g. `ng-if`) . In that very spirit, I would encourage you to further your exploration of this misunderstood language. Master JavaScript and its ecosystem and you wouldn't be daunted by any new front-end frameworks coming in your way. Goodspeed!

Where to Go From Here

Functional Programming in JavaScript

Functional Programming (FP) seems to be the in thing lately. In the discussion about Promise, I mentioned in passing that Promise is a Monad. Interested to know more about this? I would recommend:

1. Reading the excellent book by Brian Lornsdorf: Mostly Adequate Guide to Functional Programming
2. Watching the awesome companion course in Egghead IO: Professor Frisby Introduces Composable Functional JavaScript

I love the above materials so much that I compiled my own notes here: Tomy Jaya's Composable Functional JS Notes

React and Redux

This book is supposed to be a prelude to React and Redux, so it's apt for me to suggest some of the materials I found useful during my journey to learn React and Redux. They are:

1. Building Applications with React and Redux in ES6 by Cory House (A thorough and comprehensive course in Pluralsight)
2. Getting Started with Redux (Dan Abramov's free course in Egghead IO)
3. Building React Applications with Idiomatic Redux (Advanced course by Dan Abramov on building idiomatic React/ Redux app)

Writing Idiomatic Code

The best way to learn idiomatic JavaScript is to look at the style guides of big tech companies. The one I would highly recommend is Airbnb's style guide available in Github: https://github.com/airbnb/javascript. It's concise and most importantly, it explains the rationale why some styles are favored than the others.

Back to the Core

If you're not satisfied with the depth of how I explain `this` keyword and want to know more about how JavaScript's prototype works. I would recommend these JavaScript materials:

1. JavaScript: The Good Parts by Douglas Crockford (curated videos by Pluralsight)
2. Understanding ES6 by Nicholas C. Zakas
3. Eloquent JavaScript by Marijn Haverbeke

A Taste of Another Framework

We learn best through building mental models and by making comparisons and classifications. If you're interested to try another framework to strengthen your learning or if you're just purely fed up with React/ Redux, I would recommend you have a shot at VueJS. Compare and contrast the approaches taken by these 2 frameworks, pick one which better suits your or your organization's needs.

Going Native with JavaScript

The world is crazy about native apps now and guess what? Equipped with just the knowledge of JavaScript and React, you too, now can code native apps, thanks to React Native. With the hype on blockchain and machine learning, people sometimes forget how revolutionary React Native is. Don't take my word for it, try out the getting started page now!

www.ingramcontent.com/pod-product-compliance
Lightning Source LLC
Chambersburg PA
CBHW031247050326
40690CB00007B/992